Contents

junior knowledge

keeping a terrarium

by Siegfried Schmitz

Translated by
Marion Koenig

Photographs :
Angermayer (5, 13, 19, 26, 30, 37); Foersch (36, 39); Kastle (8, 41); Kahl (27); Muller (36, 40, 41); Pfletschinger (4, 17, 20, 21, 22, 29, 30, 32, 33, 34) : Schmitz (42, 43); Schrempp (4, 15, 22, 24, 32, 39); Trumler (6). Drawings : Bukard Kahl.

First published in Great Britain 1973
ISBN 0 7188 2051 7

© 1971 BLV Verlagsgesellschaft mbH, München
© 1973 English Translation, Lutterworth Press
Filmset by BAS Printers Limited, Wallop, Hampshire
Printed in Germany

Lutterworth Press Guildford and London

Ideal pets for everyone

The number and variety of animals that can be kept in a terrarium is endless. They can come in all shapes, sizes and colours. They may have scales, shells or bare skins; long tails, short ones or no tails at all. Some animals have four legs, others slide on their bellies; there are animals that burrow, crawl, swim or climb and there are even some that do a spot of gliding. When it comes to food, they can be vegetarian or carnivorous; others again may be a mixture of both. However, there is one thing that all terrarium animals have in common: they are all cold-blooded, that is to say their body temperature varies according to the temperature of their surroundings — a fact which is of the greatest importance when looking after them in captivity.

Because they are all so different, it is almost impossible to group them together except perhaps under the rather colourless heading, terrarium animals.

Zoologically speaking, terrarium animals belong to two quite different classes: the amphibia and the reptiles. These classes are subdivided into orders, the orders into families, the families into genera and the genera into species. This system of classification was originated by the Swedish naturalist Linnaeus (1707–1778). You need not, of course, memorise the scientific names which are often in Latin, but they will come in useful if, for example, you wish to order a rare animal from a catalogue, read technical books and journals, or write to a friend who does not speak your language. That is why the Latin names of the species have been added to the descriptions in the margins.

If you choose them carefully and look after them properly, terrarium animals make ideal pets, providing far more pleasure than work. You can even strike up a personal relationship with them.

You will learn a lot from them, too. Keeping a terrarium will not only stimulate your interest in all living things, it will also sharpen your powers of observation, increase your manual skill and perhaps even fan a dormant interest in scientific research. Many of nature's problems have been solved after observing these animals and many a zoologist began his fascinating career with a frog, a lizard or a tortoise when he was still a child.

About the word Terrarium

The word "terrarium" comes from the Latin word *terra* (earth) and therefore basically means a container for land animals.

Terrarium animals featured in this book

Class: Amphibia (*Amphibia*)

Order: Tailed Amphibia (*Urodela* or *Caudata*)
Family: Newts and Salamanders

Order: Tailless Amphibia (*Anura* or *Salientia*)
Family: Frogs and Toads

Class: Reptiles (*Reptilia*)

Order: Tortoises (*Chelonia* or *Testudines*)
Family: Land, Marsh, and Water Tortoises

Order: Scaly Reptiles (*Squamata*)
Sub-Order: Lizards (*Sauria*)
Family: Lizards, Geckos, Agama, Chameleons, Iguanas

Sub-Order: Snakes (*Serpentes*)
Family: Grass-snakes

European Tree-Frog
Scientific Name: *Hyla arborea*
(several sub-species)

Difference between male and female: Male's throat dark, female's whitish. Only the male croaks.

Size: Up to 5 cm.

Habitat: Central and Southern Europe; Western Asia.

Habits: Sociable, friendly, likes to climb and hop. Swims well, but only takes to the water when spawning (May). After 10–12 days the tadpoles hatch out of the spawn-clusters which are the size of walnuts. After three months the tadpoles turn into small frogs and come on land. These frogs change colour partly to match their surroundings and partly because of a change of mood.

Care: Easy and highly recommended but only in a roomy container with a well-fitting wire-mesh lid. Floor-covering: leaf mould and peat. Twigs or small branches for it to climb, later possibly also a few plants. Moisture essential (a saucer of water and spray from above). Set in the sun as often as possible. Hibernation is not easy and can be omitted.

Food: Flies, spiders, moths, caterpillars, grasshoppers, beetles; if necessary, meal-worms.

The European Tree-frog does not forecast the weather

That comic little chap, the European Tree-frog, has become so rare in Central Europe that it has had to be protected by law. Specimens, however, can still be obtained from pet-shops. Most of these Tree-frogs come from Southern Europe where they are not at present threatened with extinction.

If only there were no such things as large jam jars! Some people are still using them to keep frogs in — usually with damp, rotting moss in the bottom and fitted with fine mesh-wire lids and colourful ladders. The idea seems to be that when the frog climbs the rungs of the ladder it is forecasting good weather. What nonsense! The Tree-frog loves climbing but knows nothing about the weather. It only sits on the ladder because it likes to look down at the world from above, especially as the air at the bottom of the jar is usually pretty foul. It would much rather leave its narrow, stuffy prison for ever, but that the ignorant nature-lover will not allow. When eventually the frog's green skin turns a dull yellow, it may be almost too late to throw away the jam jar and transfer the dying creature to a bigger, more suitably equipped container.

European Tree-frog laying eggs.

Tortoises are children of the sun

Hermanns Tortoise
Scientific Name: *Testudo hermanni*

Difference between male and female: Male's tail is longer and more powerful, the underside of his shell is slightly curved.

Size: Up to 25–30 cm.

Habitat: Southern France

Habits: Undemanding, placid, rapidly becomes friendly.

Care: Very simple, in either an open-air or an indoor terrarium. Plenty of sunshine is good but there must always be some shade available. Heating is not absolutely essential except on cool days. Occasional short spells of artificial sunlight radiation may be given. A weekly luke-warm bath in shallow water recommended. Some fanatics oil the shells after bathing.

Food: Almost exclusively vegetarian. Don't just give it lettuce, vary its diet with cabbage, clover, dandelion leaves, berries, finely-chopped fruit. Some meat (worms, minced beef) is gratefully received from time to time. Sprinkle food regularly with calcium powder or codliver oil.

Similar care: Mediterranean Spur-thide Tortoise (*Testudo Graeca*) also often imported. This tortoise needs slightly more warmth.

Every year young tortoises, usually the Spur-thide variety, are sent north in their thousands to the pet shops and from there, in exchange for a small sum of money, they pass into the hands of animal lovers who are often sadly inexperienced. Tortoises are comfortable, safe and sufficiently long-lived to make ideal live toys for children — or so it is thought. In fact, the fate of the wretched tortoise is not very different from that of the Tree-frog in his jam-jar. On the day it is bought the normally long-lived creature slowly but surely begins to die — although this may take several months. Assuming they are looked after properly, however, tortoises make ideal pets for the young owner of a terrarium. On no account should they be left, as generally happens, to run freely throughout the house; not only because there is a constant danger of treading

An ideal home for a tortoise is a roomy, sunny, open-air terrarium, but some shade must always be available.

on them or trapping them in a door but, more important still, because it is much too cold and draughty for them on the floor. Tortoises come from the south and, therefore, like a warm climate. This is particularly true of young animals which have recently been acquired. They are often still babies and very delicate.

During the summer months, tortoises prefer to live in an open-air terrarium which you can build yourself out of stones or cement blocks in your garden. A square latticework cage with sides made of wire-netting, or a pen made from an ordinary flat box without a lid or base will do just as well. They can be moved across the lawn at regular intervals, so that the animals are always on a fresh patch of ground and, to some extent, can feed themselves. Make sure that the sides of the box are sufficiently high, otherwise in spite of their apparent clumsyness and heavy shells, the tortoises may manage to climb out. The lower edge should be weighted down or sunk a little way into the ground so that the inmates cannot burrow their way out. Tortoises are highly inventive and unbelievably stubborn when it comes to breaking out of captivity. Like experienced escapers, they climb on top of each other to surmount their high "prison walls".

During the colder seasons of the year, the animals should be kept in an indoor terrarium, if necessary in a plain wooden box with as large a floor surface as possible and a floor-covering of gravel and flat stones. If the terrarium is situated in a warm room and it is possible to irradiate it occasionally with an infra-red lamp, then the tortoises can be kept throughout the year without hibernating. Otherwise they must be left to winter in a cool, frost-proof cellar. On no account should they be put out of doors and left to fend for themselves in the autumn.

Two simple, practical cages for tortoises: a run made of wire-netting (*right*) and a box-terrarium (*left*).

Hibernation

Like lizards and frogs, tortoises hibernate in their natural state during winter in sheltered hiding-places. Their temperature drops sharply and their body functions are reduced to minimum. It is a good thing if the animals in a terrarium can also maintain their normal seasonal rhythm. It helps them to live longer and may even mean that they will produce offspring during the following year. If the animals should become restless in the autumn, they should be moved into a cool cellar (temperature between 2° and 8°C and established in a box containing a layer of peaty moss and autumn leaves about 30 cm deep. This layer should never be allowed to dry out completely, so check it at regular intervals and when necessary sprinkle it with water. The animal should be well-nourished but have fasted for a few days and allowed to empty its bowels completely. Set the animal in the box and watch to see if it burrows down. If it does not, don't force it. Make another attempt later on or carry on looking after it in a warm room (which in any case is better than inadequate hibernation). If the animal succeeds in hibernating it can be left alone without a qualm until spring when the sun shines warmly again. Then fetch out the tortoise and give it a luke-warm bath.

Fully grown male Mediterranean
Spur-thide Tortoise

It is easiest to tell the difference between
the Hermann Tortoise (*left*) and the
Mediterranean Spur-thide Tortoise from
behind.

If conditions are extremely favourable, a tortoise may even lay eggs. A rare event like this should naturally be crowned by an attempt to hatch the eggs and rear the baby animals. In any case some action must be taken as the mother tortoise ceases to bother about her eggs once she has laid them. In their natural surroundings they would hatch in the hot sun. In our latitudes, we must remove the eggs and hatch them out in a temperature of about 25°C. The eggs can be placed in a plastic bowl, covered, up to about one centimetre, with sand and suspended inside a warm-water aquarium, of course, in such a way that the water will not enter the bowl. After about 3 months the baby animals should hatch out — if you are lucky! The baby tortoises will, however, be particularly delicate and sickly. To survive, they will need a draught-free home, much sunshine and food rich in vitamins.

A house made to measure

Tree-frogs and tortoises do not have any special requirements when it comes to a place to live. Almost all other terrarium animals are less easy to please. Some like to climb or hop and so need a tall house; others prefer as much floor space as possible on which to stretch their legs. Some animals enjoy an occasional bathe or may even spend all their lives in the water, whilst others hate any feeling of dampness like the plague. Most animals insist on a house that is well heated and lit.

Experienced terrarium owners recognise five different types of container: (1) the unheated and dry (2) the unheated and damp (3) the heated and dry (4) the heated and damp (5) the water terrarium or aquaterrarium, which is basically only a kind of aquarium.

That sounds confusing; however, the beginner would do well to cut out the extreme kinds (such as the damp, jungle terrarium) and leave them to the specialists. The five basic types can thus be

Handling animals

Many people dislike handling a reptile, but this dislike is generally overcome quite quickly as soon as the the animal concerned has become a familiar pet. Of course that does not mean pets should be constantly handled. Most animals do not find handling agreeable. Occasionally, however, it becomes necessary to pick up your pet and then it is a great advantage if you can do so without feeling nervous or being clumsy. Ultra-cautious people wear a leather glove, although this is really only necessary in the case of specially aggressive animals (e.g. the Tuckoo or an untamed Horned Lizard). If you want to grasp an animal, advance your hand slowly and gently from the side, then quickly catch hold of the upper part of its body — but do not hold it too tightly. Never grab it by the tail — it could snap off (especially in the case of Lizards, Geckos and Blindworms). Note: You will find it easier to catch hold of an animal after the heating has been turned off and the animal has become comparatively cool.

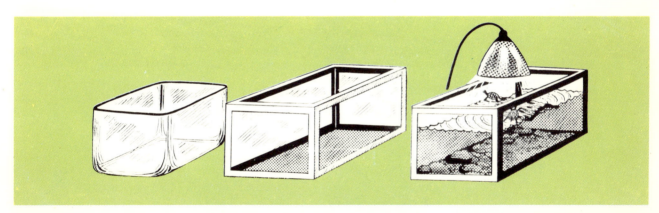

reduced to two: the many-sided box terrarium and the simple water tank. Containers for terrarium animals can, of course, be bought in any pet shop although they are not exactly cheap. The usual wire-netting covered box soon becomes too small and a bigger, glassed-in terrarium costs three or four times as much again. However, you can provide yourself with a terrarium at a fraction the cost if you make it yourself.

For salamanders, frogs and other water-loving animals, an all-glass or frame aquarium is suitable (*left*). The right hand drawing shows how a frame aquarium can be equipped to hold turtles (see also page 35–36).

How to make a terrarium

The object is to make a simple multi-purpose terrarium that can be heated, lit and have a small pool for water-loving animals. In addition, it must not cost too much, look reasonably attractive and be easy to move (in summer it is to stand in the sun). Finally, it must not be too difficult to make.

The best building material to use is wood – strong, well-seasoned plywood or blockboard about 8–10 mm thick with strips of beading of the same thickness. At a pinch, smooth chipboard will do. The advantage here is that it will not warp, but it is less suitable for use in a damp terrarium. Now the dimensions: a medium-sized container, which should suit all walking terrarium animals, would be – width : 60–70 cm ; depth : 40 cm ; height : 40–50 cm. Cut out the floor, back wall and one side wall to these measurements and join them together by sticking them with glue then securing them firmly with nails or wood screws (fig. 1). Cut a narrow board 10–12 cm wide to fit across the front and fix it to the floor and to the one side already fitted (see fig 2). The remaining side wall is made from a board of the same width and three strips of beading of matching thickness (see fig 3). In order to avoid complicated carpentry, first glue the parts together then glue and nail thin pieces of plywood onto the inside to cover the joints (see fig 4). The open part of this side wall is then covered on the inside with galvanised wire-mesh – or a plastic-covered equivalent – and the completed end glued and nailed to the box as before. Next, join the top of the two side walls by means of a strip of wood about 3 cm wide (fig 5) ; fix along the lower edge a u-shaped strip of plastic channeling and do the same along the top edge of the bottom board (see fig 6). Into these two plastic channels fit a plain sheet of glass, cut to measure with the edges ground smooth. Now, all that is left is the roof. This is also made out of wooden strips and in such a way that it consists of two frames. A sheet of glass is fixed into one of these frames (fastened on the underside by small strips of wood or upholstery tacks) ; wire-mesh covers the other – to ensure proper ventilation (see fig 7). Alternatively, both frames can be covered with wire-mesh or, if you are good at carpentry, fit a little door. The ceiling frame is then loosely laid on top (little wooden blocks should be screwed into each corner so that it can't move about).

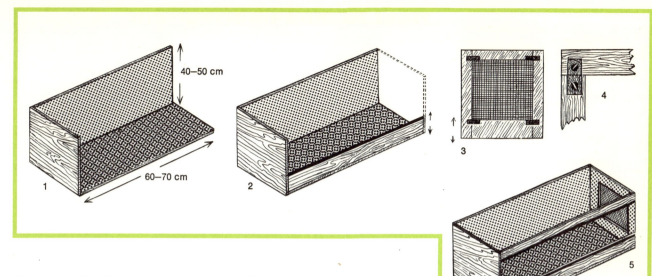

Of course the frame should completely cover the top of the container. The upper edge of the box must be planed or rubbed smooth with sandpaper (see fig 8). Finally, paint all the wooden parts inside and out – don't forget to give them an undercoat first – and then add one or two coats of varnish. The best colours to use are grey or green. That's it.

There is an alternative suggestion for all those who have, stored away somewhere, an old-fashioned, glass-fronted cupboard. This piece of furniture can be transformed into a splendid terrarium in next to no time. Just cut big openings – square, oval or round – in the top and sides and cover them with wire-mesh from the inside. In addition, a narrow strip of wood can be stuck down inside the front directly behind the glass pane to prevent whatever is used to cover the floor from falling out. Finally, the whole thing must be thoroughly painted before use.

The terrarium is finished – but where would be the best place for it to stand? A light, airy spot in the sun is naturally the one most terrarium animals like best in their natural state so, for example, choose a window-sill facing south so that the window can be opened regularly to let in sun and air. It goes without saying that whenever possible during the warmer seasons, the container should be set in a sheltered spot on a balcony, or in the garden.

Only a few terrarium animals (such as salamanders, frogs and newts) do not require their homes to be so carefully sited – they don't even mind a north-facing window and are quite happy when kept out of direct sunlight.

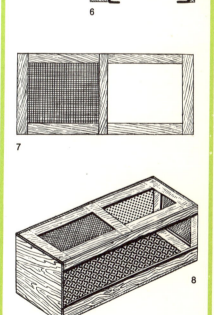

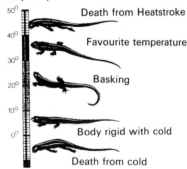

Body temperature

50° — Death from Heatstroke

40° — Favourite temperature

30°

20° — Basking

10°

0° — Body rigid with cold

Death from cold

Experiments have shown, for example, that for the Common Lizard the right temperature is more important than the brightest sunshine. If it is put in an only partly-heated container, it will always seek out the temperature that suits it best (38°–39°C) regardless of whether the sun is shining there or not. Reptiles are at their liveliest if their surroundings are the right temperature; if it is too cold for them, they soon become rigid, and if the temperature rises above what is normal for them, they suffer a heat-stroke and die. This often happens more quickly than one would think possible. The above drawing shows the different grades of lizard life and their dependence on body temperature.

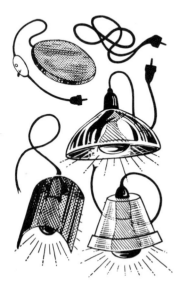

Hot-plate, element, and lamps suitable for use in the terrarium

Heating and lighting

Almost all terrarium animals, even those of local origin, need plenty of warmth and light. In summer this presents no problem; the terrarium can be placed out of doors. But take care! Too much sunshine can kill the animals if they cannot shelter in a patch of shade when they need to.

While it can sometimes get too hot for some sun-loving animals in summer, it is certainly too cold for any of them in winter, even in a heated flat. Additional heating is absolutely essential if the animals are to be kept healthy and lively. The simplest, safest and cheapest solution is a heating cable covered with a lead of plastic coating, which can be bent (but gently) whichever way you want and easily placed among the foliage on the floor or covered with a light layer of sand. And that's that! A small hole is bored through the back of the terrarium through which the cable is passed.

The heating can be kept switched on all day – a 15–25 watt element uses very little electricity – and need only be switched off when you go to bed. It does not matter if the terrarium rapidly cools down at night, for this is just what would happen in nature.

The next best solution to your heating problems would be to use a small hot-plate, provided the amount of heat can be suitably regulated. All electrical equipment must be properly insulated and comply with safety regulations.

The heating equipment will, of course, only heat part of the ground, but that is no disadvantage – on the contrary, it will enable the animals to choose a place in the terrarium where the temperature is just right for them and any kind of danger from overheating is ruled out.

Additional warmth is supplied by the electric lighting which serves a two-fold purpose: it gives the animals plenty of light and also allows us to see them properly. A practical suggestion for the home-made terrarium is a small strip-light hidden behind the upper beading at the front. More expensive lamp fittings can of course be obtained from specialist shops. Normally, you would fit an ordinary light bulb into the reflector, but occasionally this can

be replaced for an hour at a time by an infra-red bulb. Alternatively, you can make your own reflector out of an old office lampshade, a square piece of aluminium or a flowerpot lined with aluminium foil. These are all easy and cheap to make. A terrarium owner must be inventive and if you experiment you may hit on a better solution yourself.

Introducing that portly fellow the Common or Grass Frog widespread from Britain to Japan. You will find more about him on pages 31/32.

Equipping your terrarium

Sickness and Health

Reptiles and amphibia are ill more often than is generally realised. Symptoms are not usually very apparent. Fairly definite signs of internal illness are a change in behaviour, reluctance to move about and refusal to eat. Often it is a question of some food deficiency due to inexperienced treatment. Sick animals can often be saved by increasing the heating slightly, giving them a careful dosage of sun-ray treatment plus a sprinkling of vitamins and calcium on their food. You should in any case get into the habit of adding a few drops of animal vigantol or some other multi-vitamin preparation and calcium in the form of vita-chalk, Kalzan-powder, powdered Calcipot tablets or sepia pods. Animals that are seriously ill must be isolated at once in order to avoid infecting the other animals. Do not count on saving seriously ill animals. Veterinary treatment of terrarium animals is still in its infancy, and specialists with enough knowledge to be helpful are not easy to find. The most likely place to look is in your local terrarium club or the nearest zoological gardens. There is more chance of success in the case of external ailments. Skin wounds can be treated with antiseptic cream or powder obtainable from your local chemist. Inflammations or swellings can be bathed in luke-warm camomile tea; obstinate cases can be treated with a mild solution of trypaflavin or potassium-permanganate (10 mg to 2 pints of water). The best medicine, however, is to give the animal the right care in the first place: keep it clean, give it a varied diet and sufficient warmth. The age-old conflict between hygiene and a romantically naturalistic arrangement of the container should always be resolved in favour of hygiene, in other words, in favour of the animals.

Two easy-to-make food bowls for terrarium animals whose diet consists of live food and who like to get their meal-worms in a natural way (*above*). Terrarium terrace made of polystyrene (*below*).

The best material to use for covering the floor of the terrarium is a mixture of sand and gravel — make sure it is not too fine and that there are no sharp edges. However, before covering the ground, we must think about the back and side walls. You can leave them as they are if you like, but they would look more attractive covered with wallpaper. Use self-adhesive plastic-coated wallpaper with a suitable pattern (plants or stone-wall); plastic papers with patterns standing out in relief are highly suitable and provide additional climbing opportunities for the animals, but make sure you leave no gaps into which the tinier ones could squeeze. There is, of course, a more natural way of decorating the walls. Nail flat pieces of bark or plywood close together, side by side. Alternatively you could line the walls with bamboo or straw mats which have the additional advantage of being easily cleaned or changed. Set up two small branches as climbing trees and you may feel like adding one or two small potted plants to make the whole arrangement more attractive. Then cover the floor with sand and gravel, making the back slightly higher than the front. See that the flower-pots are buried up to their rims and if you want you can outline the rims with a few stones.

This sort of floor-covering, when about 10 cm deep, is quite heavy. To help support it, an additional layer of polystyrene tiles can be laid over the floor. This material is as light as a feather, easy to handle and yet keeps the floor warm. Leave openings for the flowerpots and climbing branches. Polystyrene has another advantage — you can use it to make terraces. Cut pieces of a suitable size out of a sheet of polystyrene and stick them on top of each other with a suitable adhesive. Hide the polystyrene under a thin layer of sand. To make sure it stays hidden you could paint the whole surface with glue and then cover it with sand while the glue is still wet.

Further ideas for decoration: slate-tiles, large stones, pieces of bark, tree-roots, air-bricks, etc. Imaginative landscapes containing hiding-places, climbing opportunities and sunbathing terraces can be built out of stones and cement (one part cement to three parts

Terrarium with a pool of water made out of two plastic dishes which fit one inside the other. In order to help the animals climb in and out, build a small flight of steps out of flat stones.

A pair of Wall Lizards sunning themselves on a stone.

Terrarium accessories : Feeding needle ;
atomizer ; tweezers ; spray-bottle ;
thermometer ; butterfly net.

sand) or can be modelled out of a plastic material like plaster of paris or polyfiller. Structures made in this way must be thoroughly washed with water before being fitted.

Containers for travelling

While we are on the subject of installing and arranging containers, we should spare a thought for ways of transporting terrarium animals. Sooner of later every terrarium owner will find it necessary to take or send on a journey a live lizard, frog or tortoise. This can be done quite easily and does not hurt the animal, provided that certain basic rules are followed.

It is perfectly simple to carry lizards and toads — which like to keep dry — in a small linen bag which can be closed with a drawstring and then put into a small cardboard, or better still, a wooden box. A few air-holes should be bored into the container. In the case of tortoises, we do not even need to bother with the linen bag ; a strong box, not much bigger than the animal itself, can be lined with moss or other soft material. Animals with a liking for damp conditions will travel best in a tin box which contains a small, wet sponge or piece of material but no plants ! Hammer several holes into the tin with a large nail, knocking it through from the inside

The Spotted Salamander is not at all creepy. Its expression is alert and confiding.

outwards so that there are no sharp edges for the animal to graze itself upon.

No food should be given to terrarium animals while they are travelling. In any case, they will certainly lose their appetites and a short period of fasting will not hurt amphibians and reptiles.

An owner wishing to send animals by road or rail can only do so by express delivery or, in the case of heavier parcels, express freight. And don't forget to label the package clearly: "LIVE ANIMALS, HANDLE WITH CARE".

Hints for choosing terrarium animals

The most important consideration is the animal's state of health. Healthy amphibia and reptiles are active and normally shy. Beware of apparently trusting animals which do not attempt to avoid your outstretched hand. These are not the tame creatures they appear to be and it is doubtful that they would survive the move into your terrarium. Dull or inflamed eyes, poor skin and wide-open mouth are also indications of ill-health. An animal's appetite cannot generally be observed when buying a terrarium animal. Here one has to rely on the seller's word; if the answer is evasive, it would be better not to buy the animal in question for eating habits are not easy to change. It is true that terrarium animals can survive without food for long stretches, but their health will eventually deteriorate. Animals which look either bloated or excessively fat should also be rejected. When you have finally decided on your animal, make sure you are told its exact name (the Latin one as well as the common one), its place of origin, its feeding habits and needs with regard to heat and dampness. You would do well to write these down immediately. More detailed information can be obtained from specialist books once you have settled the animal into its new home.

An old glass-fronted cupboard can easily be turned into a terrarium.

Plants for your Terrarium

In an aquarium plants are essential for the preservation of life while in a terrarium they are generally only there for decoration; attractive to the human observer, but a matter of indifference to the animals inside, unless they provide additional food or can be used for climbing. The choice and care of plants for the terrarium is a science in its own right and anyone who wants more precise information should go along to the reptile house of his nearest zoo and obtain advice from the keepers. However, the beginner is recommended to start with a relatively inexpensive selection of plants that are easy to look after. For the unheated terrarium grasses, heather, ivy and dwarf-juniper are suitable, while agave, aloe, tradescantia and dwarf-palm can be used in either a heated or non-heated container. All plants need care to prevent them from dying and they should be changed frequently — an easy matter if they are grown in flower-pots.

Anyone who wants to avoid all trouble and a great deal of expense should overcome his scruples and buy artificial plants which are available everywhere and in great variety. It is all the same to the terrarium animals whether they climb on real or plastic plants and experience has shown that the human observer can scarcely tell the difference, if the imitations are chosen with care and no outlandish, garish plants are bought. One important advantage of artificial plants is that they can easily be removed, cleaned, and put back as good as new. Finally a word of warning: although a large collection of plants does not endanger the health of your animals the effect created is far from pleasing!

The drawing (*left*) shows a selection of favourite terrarium plants which are easy to obtain. From top to bottom: philadendron, sansevieria, tradescantia, agave and dwarf-juniper.

The coloured photo (*right*) shows a dwarf chameleon which has climbed on to a high twig in order to keep a look-out for prey. Its mobile eye is probably in the act of following a flying insect.

The swift little Sand Lizard: a "reptile"

Broad-flanked and apparently completely unresponsive, it lies basking in the sunshine on a stone; but at the slightest approach of danger, i.e. as soon as its line of retreat is threatened, it flits into hiding like a streak of lightning.

The Sand Lizard is the best-known of our few indigenous reptiles. It is shy and very swift, qualities that can give you plenty of trouble if you try to catch one. Seize a lizard, and generally all you will have left in your hand is its long, twitching tail. The maimed lizard itself will have darted away long before you have got over the shock.

Should you really try to catch a lizard? It would be much better if you did not, for unless you are experienced you could hurt the creature or even kill it. Why not wait until you can buy one from your local petshop? The animals for sale in the shops are usually imported from abroad where the species is not so threatened with extinction.

The attraction of the Sand Lizard rests in the first place on its graceful shape, less on its colouring, a rather unsightly mottled grey-brown. It is only in spring that the male animals come out in a bright green skin. The breeding season starts in May.

It is very rare for lizards to produce eggs in captivity and there can

In the photograph (*right*) you can see a Sand Lizard casting its skin. The old skin comes off in great strips.
The sequence of pictures (*opposite*) shows the development of a lizard from embryo stage to the young animal hatching out of its egg.

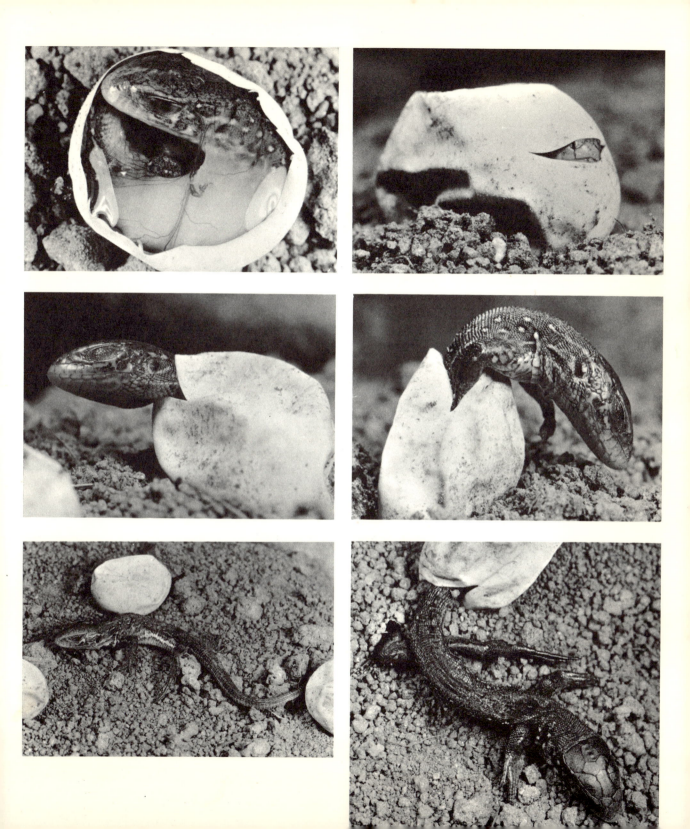

Head of a male Sand Lizard (*above, left*).
Even Green Lizards sometimes have a
fight (*above, right*).

be no chance of this at all if they have not been in hibernation
during the winter months.

Sand Lizards, and their close relative, the smaller, daintier Common
or Viviparous Lizard, are very good animals to keep in a dry,
heated, well-aired terrarium which has been turned into a replica
of our own countryside with ivy, clumps of grass and an artificial
tree-stump.

The Green Lizard and
the Eyed Lizard

Green Lizard
Scientific name: *Lacerta viridis.*

**Difference between male and
female:** The throat of the male turns
a beautiful blue in spring.

Size: 40–60 cm.

Habitat: Southern Europe. Occasionally in Southern Germany, Southern
Britain.

Habits: Dignified and quiet, but
very swift.

Care: Not very easy. Needs plenty
of light, air and warmth. Sandy floor-
covering with a place in the sun.
Opportunities for climbing.

Food: Small, live animals such as
insects, snails, spiders, smaller lizards.

These two big lizards can almost always be found for sale in pet-
shops. They have names which are perfectly in keeping with their
vivid appearance. The Green Lizard's elegant, slender body is
coloured a bright green, often with a suggestion of blue or yellow.
At first sight, the Eyed Lizard looks very similar with its bright green
skin and flanks which are covered with minute yellow and black
"eyes" or spots. Both animals are quick at running and climbing,
and they certainly require special attention with regard to housing
and food. If you have a choice, start with a Green Lizard. This

22

Green Lizard

Eyed Lizard
Scientific Name: *Lacerta lepida.*
Difference between male and female: Male more powerfully built with a squarish skull.
Size: Exceptionally up to 80 cm.
Habitat: South-western Europe.
Habits: Powerful, aggressive animal. Inclined to be fearful at first.
Care: Acclimatisation difficult. Otherwise like Green Lizard.
Food: Small, live animals such as insects, spiders, other lizards. Will also relish minced, raw meat and raw egg.

animal is smaller, cheaper and easy to look after in a terrarium you have built yourself. The gigantic Eyed Lizard, on the other hand, needs a much bigger container for, under favourable conditions, it can reach a length of about 80cm. It is the biggest lizard in Europe today. Both animals should either be kept individually, or with another reptile of the same size or a little bigger; smaller animals would not be safe from the teeth of their stronger companions — fortunately the lizard's bite is not dangerous to humans.

This is a typical habit of many lizards and provides them with a form of protection: the cast-off section of tail goes on twitching for quite some time and appears to the attacker to be a live animal and so distracts it while the reptile escapes. This kind of self-defence and self-mutilation is not very painful, although it does disfigure the animal for a time, until a new tail has grown; the second tail is, however, generally shorter and less attractive than the first one. Sometimes the first tail is not completely detached; in spite of this, a new tail will grow and, in the end, the animal has two tails. Lizards have even been seen with three tails!

Slow-worm

Scientific Name: *Anguis fragilis.*

Difference between male and female: hard to distinguish. Some older males have blue spots on their back.

Size: 40–50 cm.

Habitat: Europe.

Habits: Harmless, somewhat clumsy, very long-lived.

Care: Easy in an open-air terrarium or moderately damp, unheated container with plenty of potted plants. Fresh moss on the floor (change it frequently). Careful handling essential; the overlong tail breaks off very easily! Hibernation problematical; look after it in an indoor terrarium in winter.

Food: Worms, slugs, also all possible insects. Early morning or evening preferred as feeding time.

Similar Care: Sand Skink (*Chalcides chalcides*).

The slow-worm glides through the undergrowth just like a snake. But, in spite of its appearance, it is a harmless, little lizard which has lost its legs as part of an evolutionary process.

Slow-worms aren't snakes

Our native Slow-worm (also called Blindworm) has no visible legs (only the rudimentary ones in its skeleton indicate to which species it really belongs). Therefore it moves like a snake and is often mistaken for one. However, slow-worms are harmless, lovable creatures which do not hurt human beings in any way; on the contrary, if kept in a thickly planted terrarium, they will be a constant source of pleasure. They can even manage without heating, though they do need a certain amount of damp and shady hiding-places into which they will prefer to disappear during the daytime. During the warmer months of the year they will enjoy being transferred to an outdoor terrarium though not in the same cage as the smaller lizards which a slow-worm may sometimes mistake for its favourite food, worms. If you are lucky, you may even witness the birth of baby Slow-worms in June or July. These can be reared on small worms, snails, and other creatures. By the way, it is not only the Slow-worm's appearance which is mislead-

ing but also its other name, for any one who thinks that a Blindworm is blind is in for a shock. The world-famous German naturalist, Brehm, wrote: "The most important of the Blindworm's senses is unquestionably its sight in spite of its baffling common name. It has two attractive eyes with a golden-yellow iris and a dark centre. Whether the Blindworm can see as well in bright sunlight is another question, but here evidence of uncertain behaviour in such cases argues against it."

The Sand Skink, a distant relative from more southern countries, has actually got four tiny legs but they are so rudimentary that this animal generally prefers to slide forward on its belly. It is hardly ever seen in pet-shops, is much more temperamental than the Slow-worm and needs a warmer container.

Another animal which is not really suitable for a beginner, is the Scheltopusik or Glass Lizard, another member of the slow-worm family. It soon becomes friendly but can grow to a length of over 1 metre and therefore needs a lot of space. In addition, it is notoriously greedy and so would need a heavy diet of worms, snails, slugs, mice and lizards. What may well be too objectionable, is the prospect of feeding one inmate of your terrarium with other smaller inmates; but you should always remember that in nature animals do eat one another and we should always care for our animals in accordance with their natural needs.

Protection Laws

These do not absolutely forbid the catching of protected animals. Some animals from the following species may be taken for observation in a terrarium: **Sand Lizard, Slow-worm, European and Alpine Salamanders, Grass Snake, all frogs, toads and newts.**
However, it is recommended that such animals should be returned in the autumn to the place where they were caught, so that the number of our native animals should not decrease because of our interest in them.

A real snake for a beginner:
the Grass-snake

The budding terrarium owner should avoid all snakes at first, and especially the poisonous ones which it is best to observe through a thick pane of glass at the zoo. However, an exception can be made in the case of the native Grass-snake, which is such an established inmate of the terrarium world that we can hardly overlook it. Its care is not difficult and is possible even for a beginner, provided he can manage to overcome the opposition of all the other members of his family. A fear of snakes is a deeprooted, but wholly unfounded, fear. This handsome and completely harmless snake will soon change your relatives' cries of alarm into exclamations of admiration once they have got used to it.

Grass-snakes do not even need a heated terrarium. Instead, they welcome a fairly spacious pool as they enjoy swimming and diving. Sometimes they stay underwater for a remarkably long time. After swimming, they enjoy basking in a patch of real or artificial sunlight.

Of special interest is the process of casting its skin. For this it needs peace, warmth and an extensive bath. The snake casts its old skin in one piece; thus, one has a brand-new snake which looks as if it had just come back from the cleaners.

The best way to recognise a Grass Snake is by the two, light-coloured half-moon shaped spots on either side of the back of its head. That is the "crown" worn by snakes in the old fairy tales.

One of the most colourful European amphibians is the Spotted Salamander, seen here in the full glory of his spots. Some people are nervous of salamanders because of their garish appearance, but they are, in fact, friendly, timid creatures.

The European or Spotted Salamander loves cleanliness

The garish "warpaint" worn by the European or Spotted Salamander, which zoologists simply describe as "protective colouring" is an effective deterrent to potential enemies. Almost no animal dares approach a salamander too closely. It has an additional defensive weapon in the slightly poisonous secretion from its oral glands. However, it is basically a peace-loving creature and its skin is its chief defence. This being so do not hesitate to try your luck with one!

It needs a damp, unheated, not very light terrarium, lined with moss, stones, pieces of bark and a shallow pool. However, there is one great disadvantage in having a too thickly planted container: in the first place the plants soon begin to wither and die (and that displeases the inmate just as much as it does the owner) and secondly you will only rarely catch sight of your handsome

27

European or Spotted Salamander

Scientific Name: *Salamandra salamandra*. Two sub-species: the Eastern Spotted (*Salamandra, salamandra, salamandra*) and the Western Banded (*Salamandra, salamandra terrestris*).

Difference between male and female: Hard to determine.

Size: 20 to 25 cm.

Habitat: Central and Western Europe.

Habits: Comes out at twilight; remains hidden during the daytime; wary, often indolent. Patient and long-lived.

Care: Uncomplicated if set in a hygienic, unheated container with a pool. Spray with water daily. If fed adequately, hibernation unnecessary. **Note:** wash your hands thoroughly after handling; do not let skin secretions get near your eyes.

Food: Worms, slugs, insects of all kinds, also meal-worms. Rear on water insects, enchytraea or tubifex.

Similar Care: Alpine Salamander (*Salamandra atra*).

salamander for he is an expert in the game of hide and seek. If you want to transform your home-made terrarium into a container specially for salamanders, particular attention must be paid to hygiene; completely and carefully cover the lower part of the container with a waterproof, self-adhesive sheet of plastic-coated paper (the most natural colour is a warm green). On this put a shallow bowl of water and, for decoration, arrange a few big stones, pieces of bark and damp balls of moss which you must be sure to change frequently. Every evening spray the whole arrangement lightly with water and every few days follow this up with a thorough clean-out which, with a simple decoration like this, will be child's play. Salamanders will feel happy in these surroundings — they really don't care much about romantic landscapes — and at the same time you can watch them when they become lively in the evening and start looking for food. Perhaps they may even feel so at home that they will one day produce offspring. The female does not lay eggs like other amphibians, but lays the living tadpoles straight into the shallow water, usually in spring. These tadpoles have two pairs of legs, a tail, and gills necessary for their first, aquatic stage of development. After 3–5 months the fully-developed, scarcely 5 cm long baby salamanders leave the water and come on to the land where they will spend the rest of their lives.

Between two worlds: the Newts

Alpine Newt, Great Crested Newt, Smooth Newt, Palmated Newt.

Scientific Names: *Triturus alpestris, Triturus cristatus, Triturus vulgaris, Triturus helveticus.*

Difference between male and female: During courtship, males sport brighter colours than females.

Size: Average 10 to 15 cm.

Habitat: Europe.

Habits: Undemanding, long-suffering, generally peaceable and sociable. Remarkable powers of regeneration.

Newts live in two worlds: from March to June in the water, and the rest of the time on land. There are four European species: the Alpine Newt, the Great Crested Newt, the Palmated Newt and the Common or Smooth Newt. All four are attractive, fastidious and interesting creatures, but the most handsome one is unquestionably the Alpine Newt, a marvelously colourful chap with a blue and black marbled back and glowing orange underparts. Moreover, there are other reasons why the Alpine Newt should appeal to beginners.

When you acquire your newts in spring — either from a pond or a pet-shop — they still belong in the water, e.g. a spacious glass tank or a small aquarium on a stand must be bought (suitable containers made out of glass or plastic are not expensive). All you need inside

Newt tadpole

are a few stalks of water-plants (water-weed lasts longest) on which the newts can anchor themselves when coming up for air, a piece of cork to float on the surface and serve as a patch of dry land, and one or two decorative stones. The tank must be cleaned at least once every two weeks and the water changed. The tank must have a well-fitting wire-mesh lid.

It will not be long before you can watch the courtship display of the newts and see the female deposit her eggs, one by one, on to the leaves of the water-plants. Transfer the leaves, plus the eggs, to another tank filled with water, for the parent newt thinks nothing of eating its own offspring. After a few weeks, tiny tadpoles hatch out of the eggs and, after an interval of weeks or months, the baby newts emerge to take up a life on land.

Care: Simple, partly in a sparsely arranged, well-covered aquarium with a floating cork island; partly in an unheated, damp terrarium.

Food: Worms, slugs, red gnat larvae, tubifex. During the tadpole stage, water-fleas, small enchytraea and tubifex.

Similar Care: Various foreign newts especially the beautiful Marbled Newt (*Triturus marmoratus*) from Spain, the Japanese or Fire-bellied Newt (*Cynops pyrrhogaster*) and the Eastern Newt also called the Red Eft (*Pseudoriten ruber*) from America.

Like all newts, the Smooth Newt is a little glutton. Here he is seen swallowing a tadpole.

What is to be done if the newts spend all their time crouching on the cork float, thus showing that they cannot stand life in the water any longer (and might even drown)? There are only two possibilities. You can either transfer them to a fairly damp terrarium (or drain the water from your fish-tank and arrange moss, bark and stones inside) or you can take them back to the place where you caught them and set them free. If you choose the first alternative, then, starting in August, and after obtaining specialist advice, you can gradually reintroduce them to the water by very slowly raising the water-level half an inch at a time.

Some newts, especially among the Great Crested and Alpine variety, do not mind staying in the water all the year round.

Proudly the male Crested Newt wears his colourful courtship dress. He gets his name from his handsome jagged dorsal crest which is clearly visible in the picture.

Frogs, Toads and their relatives

The European Tree Frog is generally regarded with affection and welcomed into the home. There are, however, several other batrachians (as the family of frogs, toads and newts is called) which are also suitable for the beginner.

Extremely easy to look after and, what is more, in an unplanted or sparsely planted aquarium, are the African clawed frogs, especially the dwarf varieties which fit comfortably into a matchbox.

There are also a number of European varieties suitable for terrarium life but they need more care than the exotic clawed frogs. The brownish Common Frog and the green frog with dark spots called the Edible Frog are two of them. Both need a spacious container with a large pool which you can decorate with various kinds of grasses, moss, etc, to resemble a riverside landscape. The Common Frog, it is true, spends most of the year on land, whereas the Edible Frog, regardless of the time of year, likes to escape with a great bound into the water when danger — real or imaginary — threatens. And he can certainly not complain about shortage of excitement in his natural habitat. Even among themselves the greedy little chaps think nothing of eating smaller members of their own species. For this reason, only keep frogs of the same size together in your terrarium.

Toads, too, are handsome creatures. Some people shudder at the very name — the same people who coo over a budgerigar or fondle a dog. Perhaps the reason is that in ancient superstitions the toad has always been maligned as weird, repulsive and even poisonous. Another reason is that most people have never really had the chance to look at this creature properly. If they could just see this animal close to, without any preconceptions, and look into its beautiful deep golden eyes, they would have to admit that toads possess a beauty of their own — and anyone who has anything to do with them for any length of time will soon respond to their amiable nature and rather limited intelligence. Besides, toads are useful animals, eating many insect pests. In several countries they are protected by law.

Any one who wants to change his attitude towards toads should instal one in his terrarium — either the well-known Common European Toad, or the Green Toad with its green giraffe-like

An African Clawed Frog of the Xenopus family — always a favourite inmate of the aquarium.

Smooth Clawed Frog or Platanna, Dwarf Clawed Frog

Scientific Names: *Xenopus laevis* and *Hymenochirus* (but all species are very similar).

Difference between male and female: Female is bigger than male and has flabby lobes hanging down from the anus.

Size: 7 to 9 cm; 3 to 4 cm.

Habitat: Africa.

Habits: Undemanding, hardy, lively to the point of being impetuous, but thoroughly amiable towards each other and entirely adapted to a life in the water.

Care: Simple in an unheated aquarium that is, at the most, decorated with one or two strong plants and stones.

Food: Worms, insects, tubifex, gnat's eggs, pieces of meat and fish.

patterning, or the Natterjack which, with its rather short hindlegs, cannot jump very far. The young animals are particularly appealing, a fact which even quite hardened toad-haters have been obliged to admit. The large, handsome eyes shining up at us like gold-flecked jewels are enough in themselves to make up for the coarse, warty skin which produces a caustic, though fairly harmless, secretion. All toads soon become friendly, and, as their appetite is always good, it is not difficult to supply them with food. In fact, they are in every way easily satisfied : a floor covering of sand and peat, a hiding-place in the shape of an upturned flowerpot, a shallow bowl of water for a pool and a spraying of water in the evening, that's all they need to make them happy.

Quite different, but equally modest in their demands are two different species from Germany, the Yellow-bellied Toad from the south and the Fire-bellied Toad from the north. However, the names are misleading. There are Fire-bellied Toads with yellow underparts and Yellow-bellied Toads with red underparts. But that need not concern us much. They are both handsome, amusing, amiable and much to be recommended. They can be kept healthy and lively for years in a simple, well-covered aquarium planted with water-weed or Vallisneria and equipped with an island made of cork or stones. In their natural state, these two toads are very shy creatures, but in captivity they soon become friendly. At the

approach of potential danger they assume a curious defensive attitude: they pull in their limbs and show their brightly-coloured underparts. Many animals are fooled by this trick and think they are dead — but to human beings it merely seems funny and rather touching.

A handsome inmate for your terrarium: the Yellow-bellied Toad (*above*). On the page opposite (*bottom, left*) a pair of European Common Toads. Notice the difference in size between the male and the female. (*Bottom, right*) a Green, or Changeable, Toad.

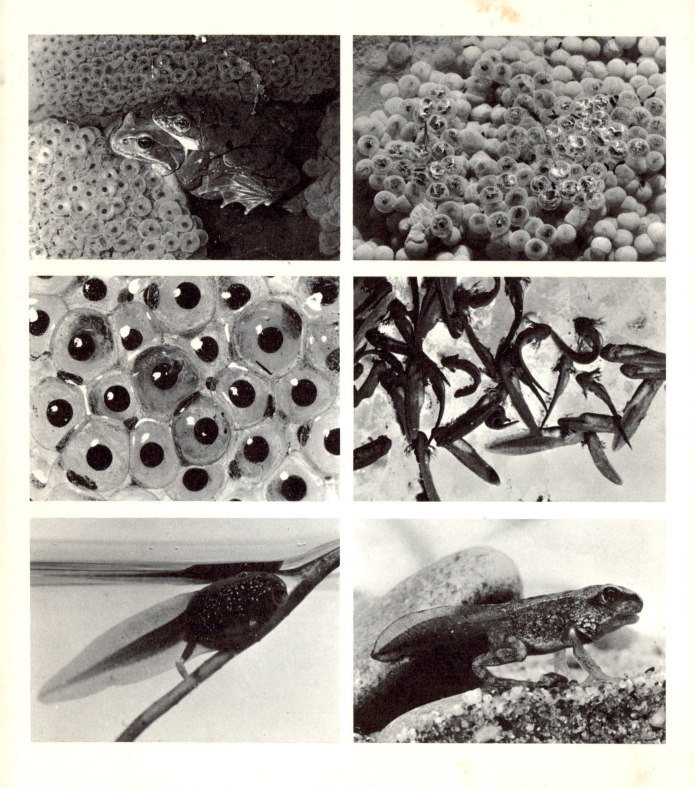

Water-loving tortoises

Water-tortoises, or terrapins, should not really be included in a book for the young terrarium owner. However, the reason they are here is because the very attractive Red-Eared Terrapins, which can be found in most pet-shops, are so liable to appeal to inexperienced customers that they instantly feel they must take a pair of them home with them. The baby terrapins, for that is what petshops nearly always offer for sale, are funny little things about the size of a 10p piece. It was obvious in the petshop that they are water animals so, when they are got home, the are dumped into a bowl of water and fed with tubifex or mealworms bought at the same time. A week later, however, the "sweet" little things are paddling about pretty listlessly in a dirty, evil-smelling pool — always supposing they can still paddle!

It is not that easy. Any one who is not prepared to go to quite a bit of trouble should leave these and other water-tortoises alone. They soon grow to quite a size and then, alas, they do tend to lose some of their youthful charm.

First and foremost, you need a spacious container and, what is more, one of the more expensive aquaria on a stand, having a metal floor with a plugged hole so that it can be emptied and cleaned frequently. The tank must, of course, be put on a high, firm stand so that you put a pail underneath to empty it. You will need to use that pail quite a lot, for turtles eat a great deal for their size and excrete a corresponding quantity. In a very short time their excrement produces such a concentration of uric acid that their eyes in particular can become damaged. There is only one solution: to change the water in the tank regularly.

Secondly, and equally essential: a water-heater — best of all, an aquarium heater with a thermostat — for the little terrapins need plenty of warmth. The heater must be firmly installed (e.g. in an airbrick of suitable size) so that the half-grown animals, strong, adventurous chaps that they are, cannot break the heater.

The third requisite is the easiest to fulfill: a patch of land for them to use when basking in the sun — a curved piece of cork cut down to fit snugly between the two sides of the aquarium. The animals will spend hours there, lying in the sunshine — which means that you must also supply either real sunshine or the artificial variety.

Red-Eared Terrapin

Scientific Name: *Pseudemys scripta elegans.*

Size: Up to 25 cm when fully grown.

Habitat: North America.

Habits: Very sociable, long-lived if given the right care; when young, lively and amusing, becoming rather more sluggish as they get older.

Care: In a spacious, heated aquarium on a stand, with an island. Regular artificial sunshine from above and approximately 1 m away.

Food: Predominantly live food (worms, meal-worms, tubifex, gnat's eggs, etc., but also pieces of raw meat and fish. Also proprietory dog food or vegetables finely shredded, particularly for older animals.

Similar care: Other species of Pseudemys and the European Pond Tortoise (*Emys orbicularis*).

The series of pictures (*left*) shows the development of a Common Frog from the egg to the almost fully-developed miniature animal, which has only to lose its tail.

A Red-Eared Terrapin is always hungry as can be seen in the picture (*above, left*). Young Red-Eared Terrapins are as attractive seen from below as from above. Unfortunately they quickly lose there lovely markings as they grow older.

An old standard lamp or table-lamp using alternately an ordinary powerful electric light bulb and an infra-red light bulb will be adequate for this purpose. The remaining decoration (sturdy waterplants, stones, etc) is a matter of personal taste — it is all the same to the animals. But take care: the less decoration the better, for absolute cleanliness is the basic requirement for the health and happiness of the inmates.

A lovable dragon: the Iguana

Coloured photograph (*right*): A fully-grown Green Iguana is an impressive sight, but it looks much more dangerous than it is.

A fully-grown Common or Green Iguana looks like a prehistoric dragon with its impressive head, its pendulous dew-lap, bizarre jagged dorsal crest, mighty clawed feet and long tail ringed with brown bands which can administer quite a hefty blow. Luckily the young animals, which can often be bought in petshops for £3 or a little more, do not have quite such a threatening appearance, but look like small, appealing lizards. Above all, their intelligent, alert eyes, make them hard to resist. Many terrarium owners have let

Green Iguana

Scientific Name: *Iguana iguana.*

Size: Up to 1·5 metres.

Habitat: Central and Southern America.

Habits: Calm, intelligent and peaceable. Quickly becomes tame.

Care: Simple in a heated terrarium with a strong branch for it to climb, and a pool. Spray with water occasionally. Regular sun-ray treatment highly recommended. Iguanas can also be allowed to run about or bask in the sun on a lawn, under supervision, in summer.

Food: When young, a mixed diet, green vegetables of all kinds, berries, bananas, cut-up, small carrots and fruits. Also worms, snails, mealworms and pieces of meat and fish. When old, chiefly vegetarian.

Similar care: Eastern Fence Lizard (*Sceloporus undulatus*), Eastern Collard Lizard (*Crotaphytus collaris*), Carolina or Green Anolis (*Anolis carolinensis*).

themselves be persuaded to try their hand at keeping an iguana for a change.

If you decide to do likewise you will not regret it, for there can be no more charming, friendly pet than the iguana. The home-made terrarium, equipped with heating, a twisted piece of branch for it to climb, a pool and perhaps one or two robust plants makes a useful home for an iguana. You can easily put two young animals together and add other reptiles of the same size and needs. The iguana will not attack them.

At first these animals are rather shy, but they quickly become acclimatized and are soon so tame that we can take them out to play with them. Some iguana owners even let them run freely about the house from time to time, without anything untoward happening to them. The only things to watch for are the long claws on their hind feet. The iguana does not intend to hurt any one but the claws are very sharp and pointed. There are many advantages to owning a Green Iguana, not least among them its varied taste in food, and only one real drawback: it grows pretty big — up to $1\frac{1}{2}$ m long (though admittedly two-thirds of this is his tail). Fortunately, it takes a long time for the iguana to reach this size and, in captivity, it hardly ever grows to the maximum length.

There are several other members of the attractive iguana family which occasionally turn up in petshops, and are just as easy to care for as the Green Iguana. Here are two of them: the dark-coloured Eastern Fence Lizard and the beautiful Easter Collared Lizard with its scarlet throat and two black bands round its neck. Both these species are considerably smaller than the Green Iguana.

Iguanas nearly all come from the new world (their old world equivalents, which are often bewilderingly like them to look at, are called agamids). The Americans have even given one of the iguanas the confusing name Chameleon. This is the graceful Carolina or Green Anolis. Needless to say there is no connection between this chameleon and the genuine chameleon, but it can also change its colour to reflect its mood, the temperature of its surroundings, or the appearance of its physical background. At one moment it is a handsome vivid green, and at the next it is coffee brown or covered in checks. The Carolina Anolis, with its oversize red dewlap, is an excellent animal to keep in a terrarium. It is a good climber and jumper and lives entirely on insects. It does, however, need a certain amount of dampness to survive.

Crack marksman and quick-change artist:
the Chameleon

Every one has heard of the chameleon and knows that it can change its colour to match its surroundings, but few people have actually seen the live animal. That is hardly surprising for chameleons are exotic animals, which, with few exceptions, live in Tropical Africa and can only rarely be seen in pet-shops. Even then it is usually only one of the chameleons commonly found in the Mediterranean.

All chameleons are grotesque creatures often with flaps of skin, protuberances, curled-up tails, and horny extensions to their noses. But they can do many things which other reptiles cannot, and by that we are not referring to their proverbial ability to change colour — several other reptiles can do that — but rather to the fantastically accurate aim of their tongues which can hit insects at a considerable distance, and their extraordinary ability to swivel one protuberant eye independently of the other. And no other animal in the world can stalk as slowly as the chameleon with its powerfully gripping prehensile toes.

They are extremely interesting animals, there is no doubt about that. However, they are also very delicate, and therefore only suitable for people who have already gained a certain amount of experience with hardier animals. Above all, you must find out from the pet-shop where the animals came from, because their need for

Chameleon

Scientific name: *Chameleo chameleon* (Mediterranean Chameleon) and other members of the family *Chamaeleonidae.*

Size: Average 20–30 cm.

Habitat: Southern Mediterranean, Africa, Madagascar.

Habits: Very slow and thoughtful, does not get on with other members of the same species. Interesting behaviour: colour-changes (chiefly due to change of temperature and/or light). Swift-moving tongue, slow-moving, independently-moving eyes.

Care: Acclimatization often difficult — according to origin in a heated and damp terrarium with plenty of opportunities for climbing (tree animal). Plenty of air important. Ventilation may need to be built in.

Food: Flying or moving prey; grasshoppers, flies, butterflies, spiders.

The two pictures below demonstrate how varied the different members of the chameleon family can be.

The head of the Jackson's Chameleon is strangely fascinating.

A dew-drop dispenser for chameleons.

heat and dampness depends very much on this. Their need for drinking water must be met not with a bowl but sprayed on to leaves to represent dew-drops. Spraying will do, but better still, use a "dew-dispenser" with a tiny hole, or a glass filled with water on the roof of the container with a thread of wool suspended from it, down which drops of water can trickle on to the leaves below. The chameleons are just as particular about their food. These super marksmen regard it as beneath their dignity to accept dead food. They specialise in flying insects and fast-moving ones at that; in an emergency, you will have to simulate flight with a pair of feeding tweezers or a needle. The chameleon will watch it with its swivel eyes then shoot out its long tongue like a flash of lightning — the only speedy thing about this animal — and just as swiftly the tongue will shoot back in with the prey attached. The prey is then chewed at leisure between the chameleon's large teeth.

Geckos, Skinks, Horned Lizards and Girdled Lizards

These lizards, like the others described in this book, are not expensive to buy, fairly easy to obtain, interesting in their habits, and both companionable and easy to look after; in short, they are suitable for a mixed terrarium in which there might also be larger lizards or young iguanas. However, it is still preferable for the young terrarium owner to have had some previous experience with reptiles.

First the geckos, and in particular the Common Gecko, which can be seen on sunny walls or rocks in Italy. The broad, rather flattened body is unmistakeable, as are the dark "soulful" eyes and the splayed-out hand-like feet which, thanks to suction pads, can grip any surface — even a vertical sheet of glass. All geckos love warmth, although they avoid the hot midday sun. They only become lively in the evening, so they are ideal animals to observe hunting for insects by the light of the infra-red lamp when you come home after being out all day.

Other members of the big gecko family are also suitable for a beginner, but anyone who wants something really rather special should obtain a Tuckoo. This impressive fellow comes from the

The two Algerian Skinks (*below, left*) look rather bewildered. They are more used to a desert landscape with plenty of sand for them to burrow in. The graceful Common Skink (*above*) won't let go once it has caught hold.

The East Asian Tuckoo is a mighty fellow who can effortlessly climb a vertical sheet of glass using the broad suction pads on his feet.

Far East, can grow to a length of 30 cm and should therefore not join the company of smaller lizards. One never knows . . .

He is also more demanding than his European fellow geckos in other ways: he loves high temperatures and strong, live food which is not always easy to find. And if you should suddenly hear barking during the night, although there's no dog in the house, then that is your Tuckoo — he has a most impressive voice, very like that of a small dog. There's another quality he has in common with some dogs — he bites, so only handle him with leather gloves.

The skinks are modest and appealing. Both the Common Skink, with its brownish or bluish crossbands and the bigger, orange-red striped Algerian Skink are the best kinds to buy. They both come from the North African desert regions and that must be taken into account when housing them. Both like to burrow into a sandy floor covering — and "swim" about in the sand like a fish in water. From the same region comes the Mastigure or Bell's Dabb Lizard which is the most commonly sold member of the Agama family. True, there are mixed feelings about it. It is not specially colourful or handsome, and it has two formidable weapons fore and aft in its broad mouth and its strong spiny tail. On the other hand, it is quickly tamed and content with a varied vegetable diet — once one has got it used to a European "prison diet". Bright yellow flowers, dandelions for example, are supposed to work wonders as appetizers. However, for safety's sake it would be better to confirm with the petshop staff that the animal you are buying is one which is already acclimatized and eating properly.

Finally, one further exotic terrarium inmate: the African Common Girdled Lizard, an animal defensively equipped with prickly outgrowths on its upper parts and tail. But here again, appearances are deceptive. In spite of its dangerous appearance, it is completely harmless. Obviously it has not much faith in its own prickles, for when it feels threatened it rolls itself up like a hedgehog in order to protect its light, soft underparts. Advanced terrarium keepers may like to try their hand with his bigger cousin, but beginners should stick to the dwarf variety which is much easier to feed and is less delicate.

We have come to the end of our little excursion into the world of the terrarium. Several highly recommended animals have been introduced: many others still wait to be discovered. The science of terrarium-keeping is a wide one in which everyone can indulge his own curiosity and ability. It is hoped that all who have read this book will now know how to go about becoming a terrarium keeper.

The Common Girdled Lizard from Southern Africa is one of the smallest animals in the terrarium.

Mastigure or Bell's Dabb Lizard

Scientific Name: *Uromastyx acanthinurus.*

Size: Up to 40 cm.

Habitat: North Africa.

Habits: Quiet; often seems sluggish; intelligent, soon becomes tame. At first often a pernicketty eater.

Care: In a well-heated container with as big a floor surface as possible. Infra-red rays. Lower temperature considerably at night. Bowl with luke-warm bathing water.

Food: Vegetarian; dandelion, clover (both with flower-heads); lettuce, cabbage, fruit, occasionally peas, cooked rice, maize, etc. Some animals also eat animal food (grasshoppers, meal-worms).

Similar Care: Other members of Uromastyx family.

Common Girdled Lizard

Scientific Name: *Cordylus cordylus.*

Size: 12 to 15 cm.

Habitat: Southern Africa.

Habits: Harmless, quiet, long-lived, mainly stays on the ground.

Care: Easy, also in a smaller, heated terrarium. Natural sunshine or artificial ray treatment.

Food: Small insects, spiders, meal-worms.

Menu for Terrarium animals

Name and Appearance	Origin	Use
Green Vegetables and Fruit 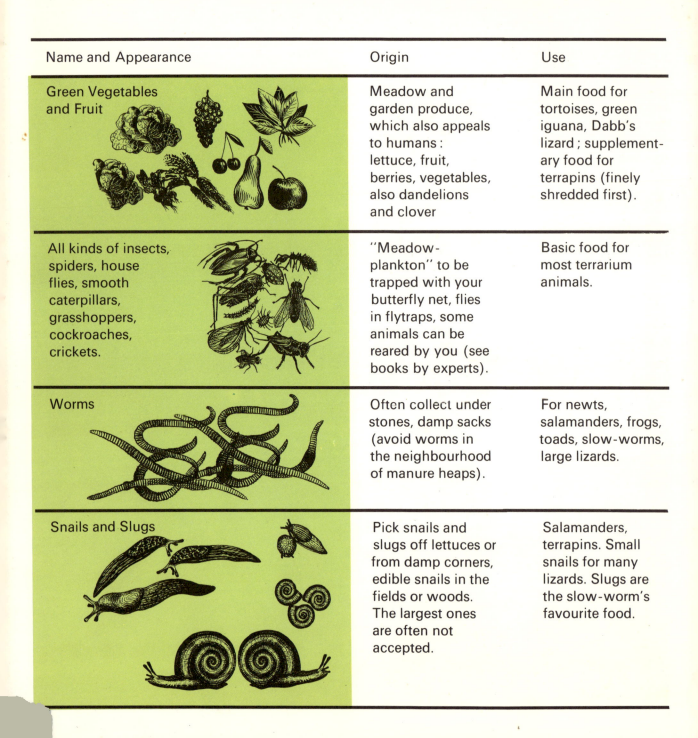	Meadow and garden produce, which also appeals to humans : lettuce, fruit, berries, vegetables, also dandelions and clover	Main food for tortoises, green iguana, Dabb's lizard ; supplementary food for terrapins (finely shredded first).
All kinds of insects, spiders, house flies, smooth caterpillars, grasshoppers, cockroaches, crickets.	"Meadow-plankton" to be trapped with your butterfly net, flies in flytraps, some animals can be reared by you (see books by experts).	Basic food for most terrarium animals.
Worms	Often collect under stones, damp sacks (avoid worms in the neighbourhood of manure heaps).	For newts, salamanders, frogs, toads, slow-worms, large lizards.
Snails and Slugs	Pick snails and slugs off lettuces or from damp corners, edible snails in the fields or woods. The largest ones are often not accepted.	Salamanders, terrapins. Small snails for many lizards. Slugs are the slow-worm's favourite food.